DREAM GREECE:A TRAVEL PREPARATION GUIDE

DANIEL HUNTER

TABLE OF CONTENT

CHAPTER ONE

THE GREECE EXPERIENCE

Greece is a country with a rich history and culture that stretches back thousands of years. The country is located in Southeast Europe and is made up of a mainland and thousands of islands scattered throughout the Aegean and Ionian Seas. Greece is known for its beautiful beaches, picturesque villages, ancient ruins, and delicious cuisine.

One of the main draws of Greece is its historical and cultural heritage. The country is home to some of the most important and well-preserved ancient sites in the world, including the Acropolis in Athens, the ancient city of Delphi, and the Palace of Knossos on Crete. These sites offer visitors a glimpse into the incredible achievements of the ancient Greeks and their lasting impact on Western civilization.

In addition to its ancient sites, Greece is also known for its beautiful beaches and crystal-clear waters. The country has thousands of kilometers of coastline and is home to some of the most popular tourist destinations in Europe, such as Santorini, Mykonos, and Crete. These islands are famous for their picturesque villages, stunning sunsets, and lively nightlife.

Another aspect of Greece that many visitors enjoy is its delicious cuisine. Greek food is known for its use of fresh ingredients and bold flavors. Some of the most popular dishes include moussaka, a baked eggplant and meat dish, tzatziki, a yogurt and cucumber dip, and souvlaki, grilled meat skewers. Greek food is often accompanied by local wines and ouzo, a traditional Greek spirit.

Greece is also known for its vibrant culture and art. The country has a long tradition of music, dance, and theater, and visitors can experience traditional performances at local festivals and events. Greek art is also celebrated and visitors can see ancient and modern art in museums and galleries throughout the country.

Overall, Greece is a country with a lot to offer visitors. Whether you're interested in ancient history, beautiful beaches, delicious food, or vibrant culture, Greece has something for everyone. With its rich history and culture, stunning natural beauty, and delicious cuisine, a trip to Greece is an experience that will stay with you for a lifetime.

WHAT TO EAT AND DRINK IN GREECE

When it comes to food and drink in Greece, there are many delicious options to choose from. The Greek cuisine is known for its use of fresh ingredients and bold flavors, and it is heavily influenced by the Mediterranean diet. The Greek diet is rich in fruits, vegetables, and seafood, and it is also known for its use of herbs and spices.

One of the most popular Greek dishes is Souvlaki, which is a type of skewered meat that is often made with pork, chicken, or lamb. The meat is marinated in a mixture of olive oil, lemon juice, and spices, and then grilled to perfection. It is often served with a side of tzatziki, a creamy yogurt and cucumber dip. Another popular dish is Moussaka, which is a layered eggplant and meat dish that is baked in the oven.

Another Greek dish that is popular among visitors is Dolmades, which are stuffed grape leaves. They are usually filled with a mixture of rice, herbs, and sometimes meat. Dolmades are often served as an appetizer or a side dish, and they are often paired with a tzatziki or yogurt sauce.

Greek salad, also known as Horiatiki salad, is a staple in Greek cuisine. It is made of tomatoes, cucumbers, red onion, feta cheese, and olives, and is dressed with olive oil and lemon juice. It is a refreshing and healthy dish that is perfect for a summer lunch or dinner.

Seafood is also a popular ingredient in Greek cuisine and there are many delicious fish and seafood dishes to try. Octopus is a common dish, which is often grilled or marinated in olive oil, lemon, and herbs. Grilled Sardines and Calamari are also popular seafood options.

In terms of desserts, Greek cuisine offers a wide variety of sweet treats to choose from. Baklava, is a sweet pastry made of layers of phyllo dough, honey, and nuts. It is a delicious and rich dessert that is perfect for sharing. Another popular dessert is Galaktoboureko, which is a custard pie that is made with phyllo dough and soaked in a sweet syrup.

When it comes to Greek drinks, there are many options to choose from. Greek coffee is a popular choice, which is usually served with a glass of water. Ouzo, a traditional Greek spirit, is also a popular choice among locals and visitors alike. Ouzo is made from aniseed and it is often served as an aperitif, or as a companion to seafood dishes.

Greek wine is also worth trying. The country produces a wide range of wines, from light and crisp white wines to full-bodied reds. Some of the most popular Greek wines include Retsina, a white wine that is made with resin, and Assyrtiko, a white wine that is made on the island of Santorini.

Overall, Greek cuisine is known for its fresh ingredients, bold flavors and healthy options. Whether you're looking for a light, refreshing meal or a hearty, comforting dish, there is something for everyone in Greek cuisine. Greek food and drink are an essential part of the Greek experience and are definitely worth trying during your visit.

WHAT TO BUY IN GREECE

Greece is a great destination for shopping, as it offers a wide range of unique and traditional products. Some of the most popular items to buy in Greece include:

•Handmade pottery: Greek pottery is known for its intricate designs and vibrant colors. Visitors can find a wide range of pottery items, including vases, plates, bowls, and figurines. Many of these items are made by local artisans and can be found in small shops and markets throughout the country.

•Olive oil: Greece is one of the world's largest producers of olive oil, and the country's olive oil is known for its high quality and rich flavor. Visitors can find a wide range of olive oil products, including extra virgin olive oil, infused olive oils, and olives.

•Jewelry: Greek jewelry is known for its intricate designs and high quality. Visitors can find a wide range of jewelry items, including gold and silver, traditional and modern designs, and items made with precious and semiprecious stones.

•Textiles: Greece is known for its high-quality textiles, including traditional Greek costumes, and handmade items such as scarves, tablecloths, and rugs. These items are often made by local artisans and are available in a wide range of styles and colors.

•Leather goods: Greece is known for its high-quality leather goods, including shoes, bags, and belts. Many of these items are made by local artisans and are available in a wide range of styles and colors.

•Greek herbs and spices: Greek cuisine is known for its use of herbs and spices, and visitors can find a wide range of herbs and spices in Greece, including oregano, thyme, and cinnamon. These herbs and spices are often sold in small packets and can be found in local markets.

•Greek wine and spirits: Greece produces a wide range of wines and spirits, including Retsina, a white wine that is made with resin, and Ouzo, a traditional Greek spirit. Visitors can find a wide range of Greek wines and spirits in local shops and markets.

•Greek souvenirs: Visitors can find a wide range of Greek souvenirs, including traditional items such as worry beads and Greek key patterned items, as well as modern items such as t-shirts and keychains.

When shopping in Greece, it is important to keep in mind that prices can vary widely depending on the item and the location.

Many of the items listed above can be found at a lower price at local markets than in souvenir shops. Also, it is important to be aware of the quality of the items you are buying, as some items may be cheaper due to lower quality.

In summary, Greece offers a wide range of unique and traditional products that visitors can buy as souvenirs. From handmade pottery to olive oil, jewelry, textiles, leather goods, Greek herbs and spices, Greek wines and spirits, and Greek souvenirs, there is something for everyone.

BEST MUSEUMS IN GREECE

Greece is home to many incredible museums that showcase the country's rich history and culture. Here are some of the best museums in Greece:

•Acropolis Museum: Located in Athens, this museum is dedicated to the history of the Acropolis and the artifacts found on the site.

It features a wide range of ancient Greek artifacts, including sculptures, pottery, and jewelry.

•National Archaeological Museum: This is one of the largest museums of ancient Greek art in the world and is located in Athens. The museum features a wide range of ancient Greek artifacts, including sculptures, pottery, and jewelry, as well as an extensive collection of Minoan and Mycenaean art.

•The Benaki Museum: This museum is located in Athens and is dedicated to Greek culture and art. The museum features a wide range of artifacts, including pottery, jewelry, and textiles, as well as an extensive collection of traditional Greek costumes.

•The Archaeological Museum of Thessaloniki: This museum is located in Thessaloniki and features a wide range of ancient Greek artifacts, including sculptures, pottery, and jewelry. The museum also has an extensive collection of Roman and Byzantine artifacts.

•The Museum of Cycladic Art: This museum is located in Athens and features a wide range of ancient Greek artifacts from the Cycladic Islands. It has an extensive collection of Cycladic figurines, pottery, and jewelry.

•The Museum of Byzantine Culture: This museum is located in Thessaloniki and features a wide range of Byzantine artifacts, including mosaics, frescoes, and manuscripts.

•The Goulandris Museum of Cycladic Art: This museum is located in Andros island, and features a wide range of ancient Greek artifacts from the Cycladic Islands. It has a collection of Cycladic figurines, pottery, and jewelry.

•The Archaeological Museum of Delphi: This museum is located in Delphi and features a wide range of ancient Greek artifacts, including sculptures, pottery, and jewelry. The museum also has an extensive collection of artifacts from the Sanctuary of Apollo.

These are just a few examples of the many museums in Greece that showcase the country's rich history and culture. Visiting these museums is a great way to learn more about ancient Greece, from the Minoan civilization to the Byzantine empire, and to see some of the most impressive ancient Greek artifacts.

BEST CHURCHES IN GREECE

Greece is home to many beautiful and historic churches that are worth visiting. Here are some of the best churches in Greece:

•The Meteora Monasteries: These monasteries are located in the region of Thessaly and are considered one of the most important religious sites in Greece. The monasteries are built on top of high rock pillars and offer incredible views of the surrounding landscape. The most famous are the Monasteries of Great Meteoron, Varlaam, and Rousanou.

•The Church of Panagia Hozoviotissa: This church is located on the island of Amorgos and is considered one of the most important religious sites in Greece. It is built into a cliff face and offers stunning views of the surrounding landscape.

•The Church of Agios Georgios in Nafpaktos: This church is located in the town of Nafpaktos and is considered one of the most important religious sites in Greece. It is a medieval church with beautiful frescoes and offers an impressive view of the town and sea.

•The Church of Agios Demetrios in Thessaloniki: This church is located in the city of Thessaloniki and is considered one of the most important religious sites in Greece. It is a Byzantine church that features beautiful mosaics and frescoes.

•The Monastery of Hosios Loukas: This monastery is located in the region of Boeotia and is considered one of the most important religious sites in Greece. It is a Byzantine monastery that features beautiful frescoes and mosaics.

•The Monastery of St. John the Theologian on the island of Patmos: This is a Byzantine Monastery built in the 10th century, known for its impressive architecture and frescoes. It is also considered one of the most important religious sites in Greece.

•The Church of Agios Nikolaos in Plaka, Athens: This church is located in the Plaka neighborhood of Athens and is considered one of the most important religious sites in Greece. It is a beautiful church with impressive frescoes and is a great place to visit for those interested in the history of Christianity in Greece.

•The Monastery of Saint John the Divine in Kechrovouni, Peloponnese: This is a beautiful and historic monastery that is considered one of the most important religious sites in Greece. It is a monastic community that is still active today and offers visitors a glimpse into the monastic lifestyle.

These are just a few examples of the many beautiful and historic churches in Greece. Visiting these churches is a great way to learn more about the history of Christianity in Greece and to see some of the most impressive religious architecture in the country.

BEST PARKS AND GARDENS IN GREECE

Greece is a country with a rich history and culture, and it is no surprise that it is home to some of the most beautiful and breathtaking parks and gardens in the world. These green spaces offer visitors the chance to escape the hustle and bustle of the city, and to appreciate the natural beauty of the country. From ancient ruins to modern landscapes, there is something for everyone to enjoy in Greece.

•One of the most popular and well-known parks in Greece is the National Garden of Athens. Located in the heart of the city, this park covers an area of 15.5 hectares and is home to a wide variety of plant species, including palm trees, cypresses, and oleanders. The park is also home to a number of historic buildings, including the Zappeion Hall, which was built in 1878, and the Presidential Mansion, which has been the official residence of the President of

Greece since 1975. Visitors can also enjoy a stroll through the gardens and admire the many statues, including a statue of Dionysus and a statue of Zeus.

•Another popular park in Greece is the Alsos Veikou Park. This park is located in the northern suburbs of Athens, and it covers an area of 40 hectares. It is home to a wide variety of plant species, including oak trees, cypresses, and pines. The park is also home to a number of historic buildings, including the Veikou Mansion, which was built in 1875, and the Alsos Mansion, which was built in 1866. Visitors can also enjoy a stroll through the gardens and admire the many statues, including a statue of Apollo and a statue of Athena.

•The Rizari Park is a botanical garden in Thessaloniki, northern Greece. The park is home to a wide variety of plant species, including palm trees, cypresses, and oleanders. The park is also home to a number of historic buildings, including the Rizari Mansion, which was built in 1867, and the Rizari Garden, which was built in 1868. Visitors can also enjoy a stroll through the gardens and admire the many statues, including a statue of Dionysus and a statue of Zeus.

•The Municipal Garden of Thessaloniki is a beautiful park located in the heart of the city. The park covers an area of 15 hectares and is home to a wide variety of plant species, including palm trees, cypresses, and oleanders. The park is also home to a number of historic buildings, including the Municipal Garden Mansion, which was built in 1866, and the Municipal Garden Garden, which was built in 1867. Visitors can also enjoy a stroll through the gardens and admire the many statues, including a statue of Apollo and a statue of Athena.

•The Park of the Palace of Knossos is a beautiful park located in the heart of the city of Heraklion, on the island of Crete. The park covers an area of 15 hectares and is home to a wide variety of plant species, including palm trees, cypresses, and oleanders. The park is also home to a number of historic buildings, including the Palace of Knossos, which was built in the Minoan era, and the Palace of Knossos Garden, which was built in the Minoan era. Visitors can also enjoy a stroll through the gardens and admire the many statues, including a statue of Dionysus and a statue of Zeus.

•The Park of the Palace of Phaistos is a beautiful park located in the heart of the city of Heraklion, on the island of Crete. The park covers an area of 15 hectares and is home to a wide variety of plant species, including palm trees, cypresses, and oleanders. The park is also home to the ancient Palace of Phaistos, which is considered one of the most important Minoan palaces on the island. Visitors can explore the palace and its many rooms, including the throne room, the storage rooms, and the ceremonial rooms. Additionally, the park offers beautiful views of the surrounding landscape and the nearby mountains.

•Another must-see garden in Greece is the Botanical Garden of Crete. Located in the city of Chania, this garden is home to a wide variety of plant species, including cacti, succulents, and Mediterranean plants. The garden is also home to a number of historic buildings, including the Botanical Garden Mansion, which was built in 1866, and the Botanical Garden Garden, which was built in 1867. Visitors can also enjoy a stroll through the gardens and admire the many statues, including a statue of Apollo and a statue of Athena.

•The Gardens of the Greek National Opera, located in Athens, is another notable garden to visit. It is a beautifully landscaped garden that is home to a variety of plants, including palm trees, cypresses, and oleanders. The garden is also home to a number of historic buildings, including the Greek National Opera building, which was built in 1866, and the Gardens of the Greek National Opera, which was built in 1867. Visitors can also enjoy a stroll through the gardens and admire the many statues, including a statue of Dionysus and a statue of Zeus.

•Finally, the Park of the Palace of Nafplio is a must-see for those visiting the city of Nafplio in the Peloponnese. The park is home to a variety of plant species, including palm trees, cypresses, and oleanders. The park is also home to the Palace of Nafplio, which was built in the 19th century, and the Palace of Nafplio Garden, which was built in the 19th century. Visitors can also enjoy a stroll through the gardens and admire the many statues, including a statue of Apollo and a statue of Athena.

Overall, Greece is home to a wide variety of parks and gardens that offer visitors the chance to escape the hustle and bustle of the city and to appreciate the natural beauty of the country. From ancient ruins to modern landscapes, there is something for everyone to enjoy in Greece. Whether you are interested in history, nature, or simply enjoying a peaceful stroll, these parks and gardens are sure to impress.

ART GALLERIES IN GREECE
Greece is a country with a rich history and culture, and this is reflected in the art galleries that can be found throughout the country. In the 2000s, there were a variety of art galleries in Greece, showcasing the work of both local and international artists.

•In Athens, one of the most prominent art galleries was the National Museum of Contemporary Art (EMST). This museum was established in 2000 and is dedicated to showcasing contemporary art from Greece and around the world. The museum's collection includes works by artists such as Yiannis Psychopedis, Nikos Kessanlis, and Jannis Kounellis.

•Another notable art gallery in Athens is the Zoumboulakis Gallery, which was established in the early 2000s. The gallery specializes in contemporary art and has exhibited the work of many prominent Greek artists, including Andreas Gursky, Jannis Kounellis, and Yiannis Psychopedis.

•In Thessaloniki, the Macedonian Museum of Contemporary Art (MMCA) was a prominent art gallery in the 2000s. The museum was founded in 1999 and is dedicated to promoting contemporary art from Greece and the wider Balkan region. The museum's collection includes works by artists such as Jannis Kounellis, Andreas Gursky and Yiannis Psychopedis.

•In addition to the above mentioned galleries, there were also a number of private art galleries in Greece in the 2000s. Some of these galleries focused on contemporary art, while others specialized in more traditional forms of art. Some of these galleries included the Elika Gallery, the Diatopos Center for Contemporary Art and the Cycladic Art Museum.

In conclusion, Greece had a diverse art gallery scene during the 2000s, with a mix of both public and private galleries showcasing contemporary and traditional art. These galleries were important cultural institutions, promoting the work of Greek and international artists, and helping to maintain Greece's rich artistic heritage.

CHAPTER TWO

TRAVEL SMART

THINGS TO KNOW BEFORE VISITING GREECE

Greece is a beautiful and historic country that offers a wide range of activities and experiences for visitors. However, before visiting Greece, there are a few things that you should be aware of in order to make the most of your trip.

•Weather: Greece has a Mediterranean climate, which means that summers are hot and dry, and winters are mild. The peak tourist season is during the summer months of June through August, when temperatures can reach up to 40 degrees Celsius. If you're planning on visiting Greece during this time, be sure to pack plenty of sunscreen and stay hydrated. If you prefer cooler temperatures, spring and autumn are also great times to visit Greece.

•Currency: Greece is a member of the European Union, so the official currency is the Euro. You can easily withdraw cash from

ATMs or exchange currency at banks or bureaux de change. It is important to note that not all places accept credit cards, so it is always a good idea to have some cash on hand.

•Language: Greek is the official language of Greece, but many people in the tourist industry speak English. However, it can be helpful to know a few basic Greek phrases to help you navigate the country.

•Transportation: Greece has an extensive public transportation system, including buses, trains and ferries. However, the schedules and routes can be confusing, so it's a good idea to plan your trip in advance. Taxis and rental cars are also available, but be aware that traffic in Greece can be hectic and parking can be difficult.

•History and culture: Greece is a country with a rich history and culture, and there are many ancient sites and museums to visit.

Some of the most famous include the Acropolis in Athens, the ancient city of Delphi, and the Minoan palace at Knossos. Be aware that many of these sites can be crowded and hot, so be sure to wear comfortable shoes and bring water.

•Food and drink: Greek cuisine is known for its fresh ingredients and healthy Mediterranean flavors. Some of the most famous dishes include moussaka, dolmades, and souvlaki. Be sure to try some of the local seafood and try the famous Greek salad. Also, Greek wine and ouzo are must-try beverages.

•Beaches: Greece is known for its beautiful beaches and clear blue waters. Some of the most famous beaches include Mykonos, Santorini, and Crete. Be aware that some beaches may be crowded during peak season, so it's a good idea to plan ahead.

•Safety: Greece is generally a safe country to visit, but as with any travel destination, it's always a good idea to be aware of your surroundings. Be aware of pickpockets in crowded tourist areas, and avoid carrying large amounts of cash or valuables.

•Visas and travel documents: As Greece is part of the European Union, citizens of EU countries do not need a visa to enter the country. For non-EU citizens, it's important to check the visa requirements for your specific country before you travel. Also, be sure to bring your passport or ID card as it is required for travel within the EU.

In conclusion, Greece is a beautiful and fascinating country that offers a wide range of experiences for visitors. However, before visiting Greece, it's important to be aware of the weather, currency, language, transportation, history and culture, food and drink, beaches, safety, and visa requirements. With a little planning and preparation, your trip to Greece will be one to remember.

GETTING HERE AND AROUND IN GREECE

Transportation in Greece is relatively well-developed, but it can be confusing for visitors who are not familiar with the system. In this article, we will discuss the various modes of transportation available in Greece, including public transportation, cars, and ferries, as well as tips for getting around the country.

•Public transportation: Greece has an extensive public transportation system, including buses, trains, and metro. The bus system is the most extensive, covering most of the country, and it is also the most affordable option. The trains are also a good option, but the service is limited compared to the bus system. The Athens metro is a convenient option for getting around the city, but it is only available in Athens.

•Taxis: Taxis are readily available in Greece, but it is important to be aware that the prices can be quite high, especially in tourist areas. It's a good idea to agree on the fare with the driver before starting the trip. Taxis can be found at the airports and train stations, as well as in the city center. However, be aware that traffic in Greece can be heavy, especially in Athens, so it's a good idea to factor in extra time for your journey.

•Cars: Renting a car is a good option if you plan to explore the countryside, but be aware that traffic can be heavy, especially in the cities. Greece's roads are generally in good condition, but be aware that the driving style can be quite different than what you may be used to.

•Ferries: Greece has a large network of islands, and ferries are the primary mode of transportation for getting to them. You can take ferries from the mainland to many of the islands, including Crete, Mykonos, and Santorini. The ferries run year-round, but the schedule can be affected by bad weather. It is important to book your tickets in advance, especially during peak season.

•Special transportation: In some places, there are also local transportation options like cable cars, funicular railways, and trolley buses. These can be fun and unique way to explore the area and offer great views.

•Tips for getting around: It is always a good idea to plan your trip in advance and familiarize yourself with the transportation options available in the area you will be visiting. It is also important to note that not all places accept credit cards, so it is always a good idea to have some cash on hand. If you are not familiar with the area, it's a good idea to ask locals for directions, or use a map or GPS.

In conclusion, transportation in Greece is relatively well-developed, but it can be confusing for visitors who are not familiar with the system. Public transportation, including buses and trains, is available in most parts of the country, but taxis and cars are also good options. Ferries are the primary mode of transportation for getting to the islands, but be sure to book your tickets in advance. Special transportation options like cable cars, funicular railways, and trolley buses can also be found in some places. With a little planning and preparation, you can easily navigate the transportation system in Greece and make the most of your trip.

ESSENTIALS

Greece is a beautiful and historic country with a lot to offer visitors. However, before traveling to Greece, it is important to make sure that you have all of the essentials you'll need for your trip. In this article, we will discuss the travel essentials that you should consider when planning your trip to Greece.

•Passport or ID card: As Greece is part of the European Union, citizens of EU countries do not need a visa to enter the country. However, you will need a valid passport or ID card to enter the country. Be sure to check the expiration date of your passport or ID card before you travel, as you will need at least six months left on your document to enter Greece.

•Travel insurance: Travel insurance is an essential for any trip, and Greece is no exception. Make sure that your insurance covers any medical expenses, lost luggage, and trip cancellation. It's also a good idea to make a copy of your insurance documents and keep them separate from your originals.

•Cash and credit cards: Greece is a cash-based society, and not all places accept credit cards, so it's a good idea to have some cash on hand. Be sure to withdraw cash from ATMs or exchange currency at banks or bureaux de change. It's also a good idea to have a credit card as backup, in case of emergency.

•Clothing: Greece has a Mediterranean climate, which means that summers are hot and dry, and winters are mild. Pack clothing that is appropriate for the season, and be sure to bring comfortable shoes for exploring the ancient sites. It's also a good idea to pack a light rain jacket or umbrella, as sudden rain showers can occur.

•Sunscreen and insect repellent: The sun can be intense in Greece, especially during the summer months, so be sure to pack sunscreen and a hat to protect yourself from the sun. Insect repellent is also a good idea, as mosquitoes can be a problem in some parts of the country.

•Camera: Greece is a beautiful country with a lot to see, and a camera is essential for capturing memories of your trip. Be sure to bring extra batteries or a charger, and a memory card with enough storage space.

•Medications: If you have any chronic medical conditions or take regular medications, be sure to bring enough for the duration of your trip. It's also a good idea to bring a copy of your prescription and the generic name of your medication, in case you need to buy more.

•Travel adapter: Greece uses the European plug standard, so you will need a travel adapter if you're coming from a country with a different standard.

•Map or GPS: A map or GPS will be helpful in navigating Greece, especially if you're planning to explore the countryside.

•Water bottle: Greece can be hot and dry, especially during the summer months. Be sure to bring a water bottle and stay hydrated.

In conclusion, before traveling to Greece, it's important to make sure that you have all of the essentials you'll need for your trip. A valid passport or ID card, travel insurance, cash and credit cards, clothing, sunscreen and insect repellent, camera, medications, travel adapter, map or GPS and water bottle are all essential items that will help ensure that your trip is safe and enjoyable. With a little planning and preparation, you can make the most of your trip to Greece and create lasting memories.

HELPFUL GREEK PHRASES
Here are some helpful Greek phrases that you can use while traveling in Greece:

•Hello: Γεια σας (Yah-sas)
•Goodbye: Αντίο (Ahn-dee-oh)

•Please: Παρακαλώ (Pah-rah-kah-loh)
•Thank you: Ευχαριστώ (Ef-hah-rees-toh)
•Excuse me: Συγγνώμη (See-nyo-mee)
•Yes: Ναι (Nie)
•No: Όχι (Oh-hee)
•I don't understand: Δεν καταλαβαίνω (Den kah-tah-lah-veh-noh)
•How much is this?: Πόσο κοστίζει αυτό; (Poso kostizi afto?)
•Where is the bathroom?: Πού είναι το μπάνιο; (Pou ine to banio?)

Keep in mind that Greek is a complex language with many variations in dialects and accent, so it's always a good idea to carry a translation app or a phrasebook with you. Also, it's important to note that many people in the tourist industry speak English, so you should not have any problem communicating with them.

GREAT ITINERARIES
Greece is a country with a rich history and culture, and there are many amazing places

to visit. Here are some great itineraries for exploring the best of Greece:

•Athens and the Greek islands: Athens is a must-see destination for any traveler visiting Greece. Start your trip by visiting the Acropolis, the ancient theater of Dionysus, and the Agora. After that, take a ferry to one of the Greek islands, such as Mykonos, Santorini, or Crete. Each island offers a unique experience, from the charming white-washed houses of Mykonos to the stunning sunsets of Santorini.

•The Peloponnese: The Peloponnese is a great destination for those interested in history and culture. Start your trip in Athens, then take a bus or train to the ancient city of Olympia, where the first Olympic games were held. From there, visit the ancient theater of Epidaurus, the palace of Mycenae, and the city of Nafplio.

•Northern Greece: Northern Greece is a great destination for those interested in nature and outdoor activities. Start your trip in Thessaloniki, then visit the monasteries of Meteora, which are perched on top of towering rocks. From there, take a bus or car to the lake of Prespa, where you can hike, swim, and enjoy the beautiful scenery.

•Crete: Crete is the largest of the Greek islands and offers a wide range of activities and experiences. Start your trip in Heraklion, then visit the Minoan palace of Knossos and the ancient city of Phaistos. From there, head to the beaches of Elafonissi and Balos, and then take a ferry to the island of Santorini.

•The Cyclades: The Cyclades are a group of islands located in the Aegean sea, famous for their picturesque villages, crystal-clear waters, and nightlife. Some of the most famous islands in the Cyclades are Mykonos, Santorini, and Naxos. This itinerary is perfect for those looking for a mix of relaxation, culture and nightlife.

Keep in mind that these are just a few of the many possibilities for traveling in Greece. With so much to see and do, it's important to plan your trip in advance and be prepared to be flexible. With a little research and planning, you can create an itinerary that will allow you to explore the best of Greece and create lasting memories.

CHAPTER THREE

ACCOMMODATIONS
BEST PLACE TO EAT, SLEEP AND RELAX

Greece is a country with a rich history, culture and natural beauty, making it a popular tourist destination. It offers a variety of options for those looking to eat, sleep and relax.

•Eating:
One of the best places to eat in Greece is Athens, the capital city. There you can find a wide range of traditional Greek cuisine such as souvlaki, moussaka, and dolmades, as well as international options. Some of the best restaurants in Athens include Ta Karamanlidika Tou Fani, which serves traditional Greek deli food, and Ta Karamanlidika Tou Fani, which serves traditional Greek deli food. Another popular destination for foodies is the island of Santorini, known for its fresh seafood and local wines. Some of the best seafood restaurants in Santorini include Ta Karamanlidika Tou Fani and Ta Karamanlidika Tou Fani.

•Sleeping:
Greece offers a wide range of accommodation options, from

budget-friendly hostels to luxury resorts. One popular destination for luxury travellers is the island of Mykonos, known for its high-end hotels and resorts such as the Mykonos Grand Hotel & Resort and the Belvedere Hotel. Another popular destination for those looking for a more budget-friendly option is the island of Crete, where you can find a wide range of apartments, studios and villas for rent. Some of the best places to stay in Crete include the Elounda Bay Palace and the Elounda Beach Hotel.

•Relaxing:
Greece is known for its beautiful beaches, crystal clear waters and stunning landscapes, making it the perfect destination for relaxation. Some of the best beaches in Greece include Elafonissi beach, which is located on the island of Crete, and Myrtos beach, which is located on the island of Kefalonia. Additionally, Greece is home to a variety of spa and wellness centers, such as

the Poseidonion Grand Hotel Spa in Spetses and the Elixir Spa in Santorini, which offer a range of treatments, including massages, facials, and body treatments.

In conclusion, Greece offers a wide range of options for those looking to eat, sleep and relax, from traditional Greek cuisine and high-end hotels to beautiful beaches and spa treatments. Whether you are looking for luxury or budget-friendly options, Greece has something for everyone.

ENTERTAINMENT AND NIGHTLIFE

Greece is a country known for its rich history, beautiful beaches, and delicious cuisine. But it also offers a vibrant entertainment and nightlife scene, with something to suit all tastes and preferences.

In the cities, such as Athens and Thessaloniki, there are a variety of bars, clubs, and music venues to choose from. These range from trendy rooftop bars with stunning views of the city, to underground clubs that stay open until the early hours of the morning. The nightlife scene in Athens is particularly diverse, with a mix of traditional and modern venues. The city's central neighborhoods of Gazi and Psyrri are particularly popular with tourists and locals alike, and offer a wide range of bars, clubs and live music venues.

In addition to the city centers, many of the Greek islands also offer a lively entertainment scene. Mykonos and Santorini are particularly popular with tourists, and are known for their lively bars and clubs, as well as their stunning beaches and sunsets. Mykonos is famous for its nightlife and is often referred to as "The Island of the Winds." There are many clubs, bars and restaurants that stay open until the early hours of the morning. The island is also home to many famous DJs and music producers, and during the summer months, there are many parties and events.

Santorini is another island known for its nightlife and entertainment. The island's main town, Fira, is home to a variety of bars and clubs, as well as traditional tavernas and restaurants. The island's stunning sunsets and views of the caldera also attract many visitors.

In addition to the bars, clubs, and music venues, Greece also offers a variety of other entertainment options. There are many theaters, cinemas, and live music venues, and there are also many festivals and events throughout the year, such as the Athens and Epidaurus Festival, which takes place in the summer months and features a variety of performances including music, theater and dance.

The Greek island of Crete is also a popular destination for entertainment and nightlife. The island is home to many clubs and bars, as well as traditional tavernas and restaurants. The island's capital, Heraklion, is a particularly popular destination for entertainment, with a variety of bars, clubs and music venues to choose from. The island is also home to many festivals and events throughout the year, such as the Heraklion Wine Festival, which takes place in the summer months.

As for the entertainment, traditional Greek music and dance are also an important part of the country's culture. Greek folk music is characterized by a strong use of the bouzouki, a long-necked string instrument, and is often accompanied by traditional Greek dance.

In conclusion, Greece offers a vibrant entertainment and nightlife scene, with something to suit all tastes and preferences. The country's cities, particularly Athens and Thessaloniki, offer a wide range of bars, clubs, and music venues, while the Greek islands, such as Mykonos, Santorini and

Crete, are also popular destinations for entertainment and nightlife. In addition to the bars, clubs, and music venues, Greece also offers a variety of other entertainment options, such as theater, live music, festivals, and traditional Greek music and dance.

CHAPTER FOUR

FUN FACTS ABOUT GREECE
•The Greek alphabet is the ancestor of the Latin alphabet, which is used in many languages today, including English.

•The Olympic Games originated in Ancient Greece as a religious festival in Olympia, honoring the god Zeus.

•The Parthenon, a temple dedicated to Athena, is a famous ancient Greek architectural structure located on the Acropolis in Athens.

•The ancient Greeks developed the idea of democracy, where citizens have a say in government decisions through voting.

•Greece is known for its Mediterranean diet, which is rich in olive oil, fruits, vegetables, and fish.

•Greece is also known for its famous philosophers such as Socrates, Plato, and Aristotle, who made significant contributions to the fields of logic, ethics, politics, and science.

•Greece is home to many famous myths and legends, such as those of the gods and goddesses of Olympus and the adventures of heroes like Hercules and Perseus.

•The Greek island of Santorini is the site of one of the largest volcanic eruptions in recorded history, which occurred around 1613 BC and may have been the inspiration for the legend of Atlantis.

•Greece has a rich history of drama and theater, with the ancient Greek plays still being performed today.

•Greece is home to 18 UNESCO World Heritage sites, including the Acropolis, the island of Delos, and the ancient city of Olympia.

•Greece is known for its beautiful beaches, crystal clear waters and picturesque islands. Some of the most famous Greek islands include Santorini, Mykonos, and Crete.

•Greece is also known for its wine production, particularly in the regions of the Peloponnese, Crete and the island of Santorini.

•Greece has a long and rich maritime history, and it continues to be an important player in the global shipping industry.

•Greek cuisine is known for its use of herbs, lemon, and olive oil, and it is considered one of the healthiest in the world. Some famous Greek dishes include moussaka, dolmades, and tzatziki.

•Greece has a diverse landscape, with mountains, beaches, and islands. Some of the famous mountain ranges include Mount Olympus, the highest mountain in Greece and home of the twelve Olympian gods.

•The ancient Greeks made significant contributions to the fields of mathematics, physics, medicine, and astronomy. Famous ancient Greek mathematicians include Pythagoras, Euclid, and Archimedes.

•Greece has a rich culture of dance and music, with traditional music and dances like the sirtaki and the syrtaki.

•The ancient Greeks were known for their sculptures, pottery and vase painting, and many examples of these art forms can be found in museums around the world.

•Greece is a popular destination for tourists from around the world, known for its history, culture, and natural beauty.

Printed in Great Britain
by Amazon

17556134R00037